M000282615

# Why I Live in
# TENNESSEE

# 101 Dang Good Reasons
## Ellen Patrick

ISBN 1-58173-290-2

Jacket and text design by Miles G. Parsons
Compiled with help from John Paul Keith
Printed in Italy

10 9 8 7 6 5 4 3 2 1

# 1. No income tax.

# 2. The Smoky Mountains.

# 3. We don't have a state song, we have a state full of song.

# 4. Sun Records.

—⁂—

# 5. The Grand Ole Opry.

# 6. Grandma's grits.

—◊◊◊—

# 7. Certain small towns that distill certain beverages.

# 8. The Pyramid in Memphis.

—⁂—

# 9. The Parthenon in Nashville.

# 10. Home of the world's largest continuous yard sale.

# 11. Two kinds of moonshine.

—∞—

# 12. Front porches.

# 13. Screen doors.

—◆—

# 14. Davy Crockett.

## 15. Daniel Boone.

—⁓—

## 16. We founded Texas.

17. Around here, the waltz never went out of style.

—⁓—

18. Second and third helpings considered the polite thing to do.

19. You can be city folk. You can be country folk. Or you can be both.

# 20. "Tennessee" makes a great pseudonym.

—⁓—

# 21. Graceland.

# 22. Tina Turner.

—⁂—

# 23. Hard to say which is bigger here, the hair or the boots.

# 24. Who else has a Mule Day Festival?

# 25. RCs and Moon Pies.

# 26. Barns that say "See Rock City."

—⟋⟍—

# 27. Rock City.

# 28. Dolly Parton.

—◊—

# 29. Dollywood.

# 30. Dolly Everything.

# 31. Maybe we didn't invent electricity, but we sure did bring it to the Tennessee Valley.

# 32. Sundays are saved for The Lord and the Vols.

—◆◆◆—

# 33. Chicken 'n' dumplin's.

# 34. Evening cricket serenades.

—⁂—

# 35. Mississippi mud.

# 36. Ryman Auditorium.

# 37. The Peabody Hotel ducks.

—m—

# 38. It makes us feel good to have the blues.

# 39. We're working for world peace through country music.

# 40. If any other state ever runs out of NASCAR fans, we got plenty here.

—⁂—

# 41. Redbud trees.

# 42. Fig preserves.

# 43. Lady Vols.

# 44. Hillbillies.

—⁂—

# 45. Fireflies.

# 46. Beale Street.

—⁕—

# 47. Lower Broad.

# 48. Trips to car dealerships minimized by number of previously owned vehicles conveniently available curbside.

# 49. "I'm from Tennessee" always impresses (and slightly intimidates) Yankees.

50. Sweet tea.

—⚬—

51. Pecan pie.

# 52. Homemade biscuits.

# 53. Barbecue.

—⁂—

# 54. The mighty Vol Navy.

# 55. No "Atkins friendly" menus.

—⌇—

# 56. Tailgating.

# 57. A missing tooth can be a fashion statement.

# 58. The phrase "Hey, watch this!" always heralds free entertainment.

# 59. Mom and Pop "restraunts."

—∞—

# 60. The lottery. It could happen.

# 61. 865 area code spells "Vol."

62. In other states you can get something for a song; in Tennessee you can get a song for nothing.

# 63. All the orange with none of the Florida.

## 64. There's a Cracker Barrel at every exit.

—⁓—

## 65. Wild honeysuckle.

66. It's always nice when your mayor can also cut your hair.

# 67. Tennessee Walking Horses.

# 68. Tomato sandwiches.

—◇—

# 69. Free states.

# 70. Mud Island.

—ɯ—

# 71. Ruby Falls.

# 72. The only state both close enough to and far enough away from Atlanta.

# 73. Drive-through windows at guitar shops.

74. A log may be used for home construction and as a bumper.

# 75. Even fancy restaurants have breakfast on their dinner menus.

# 76. Cowboy boots never excluded from formal wear.

# 77. Size matters for trucks only.

78. Lowest rate of skin cancer due to ample shade provided by the cowboy hat.

# 79. Even strangers say "Howdy."

80. More storytellers
per square mile than
in any other state.

81. We're the reason God made stringed instruments.

—∞—

82. If it's not on I-40, it's probably not in Tennessee.

# 83. Rafting on the Nantahala.

—◇—

# 84. Porch swings.

# 85. Home of three U.S. presidents.

# 86. Honking your car horn is a form of political dissent.

87. If you heard a song you like on TV, 10 to 1 it came out of Tennessee.

# 88. Lynchburg lemonade.

—⸰—

# 89. Goo Goo Clusters.

# 90. Tennessee Titans.

---

# 91. The meaning of the word "buggy" is expanded to include grocery carts.

# 92. The Tennessee River.

—〰—

# 93. Fresh water fishing.

# 94. Misty mountain mornings.

—◊◊◊—

# 95. Procrastination is widely accepted (and respected).

# 96. Riding lawn mowers are street legal.

# 97. The Chattanooga Choo-Choo.

—⁓—

# 98. If the bank forecloses on your home, you can drive it to Kentucky.

# 99. Hayrides are considered a form of carpooling.

# 100. This ain't Arkansas.

# 101. You can leave Tennessee, but you'll always come home again.